NEPTUNE

by L. L. Owens

The Child's World®

Published by The Child's World®
1980 Lookout Drive • Mankato, MN 56003-1705
800-599-READ • www.childsworld.com

ACKNOWLEDGMENTS
The Child's World®: Mary Berendes, Publishing Director
The Design Lab: Design and production
Red Line Editorial: Editorial direction

PHOTO CREDITS
NASA/courtesy of nasaimages.org, cover, 1, 3, 5, 6, 12, 14, 18, 19, 20, 21,
23, 24, 25, 27, 29, 31, 32; NASA/courtesy of nasaimages.org/The Design
Lab, 6, 7, 9; NASA/Goddard Space Flight Center Scientific Visualization
Studio/courtesy of nasaimages.org, 11; Dr. Scott M. Lieberman/AP Images,
13; The Print Collector/Photolibrary, 15; Brandon Bourdages/Shutterstock
Images, 17

LIBRARY OF CONGRESS CATALOGING-IN-PUBLICATION DATA
Owens, L. L.
  Neptune / by L.L. Owens.
    p. cm.
  Includes bibliographical references and index.
  ISBN 978-1-60954-385-3 (library bound : alk. paper)
  1. Neptune (Planet)—Juvenile literature. I. Title.
  QB691.O94 2011
  523.48—dc22
                                    2010039962

Printed in the United States of America
Mankato, MN
December, 2010
PA02072

ON THE COVER
This image of Neptune
was taken by the *Voyager 2*
spacecraft in 1990.

Table of Contents

Neptune and the Solar System

Pretend you are a space traveler. Your spacecraft left Earth 12 years ago. Look out your window. See that shiny sea-blue ball floating in space? That's Neptune!

Neptune is one of our space neighbors in the **solar system**. At the center of our solar system is the sun. Planets **orbit**, or go around, the sun.

Neptune is surrounded by
blue clouds.

SUN

Mercury

Venus

Earth

Mars

Ceres

Jupiter

Fun Facts

PLANET NUMBER: Neptune is the eighth planet from the sun.

DISTANCE FROM SUN: 2.8 billion miles (4.5 billion km)

SIZE: Neptune is about 96,700 miles (155,600 km) around its middle. That is almost four times bigger than Earth's middle.

OUR SOLAR SYSTEM: Our solar system has eight planets and five **dwarf planets**. Pluto used to be called a planet. But in 2006, scientists decided to call it a dwarf planet instead. Scientists hope to discover even more dwarf planets in our solar system!

Our Solar System

Saturn

Uranus

Neptune

Pluto

Haumea

Makemake

Eris

Planet

Dwarf Planet

While orbiting the sun, a planet spins like a top. Each planet spins, or rotates, on its **axis**. An axis is an imaginary line that runs through the planet from top to bottom.

One full spin on its axis equals one day. Think of one day on a planet as the time from one sunrise to the next sunrise. An Earth day is 24 hours. A day on Neptune is 16 hours.

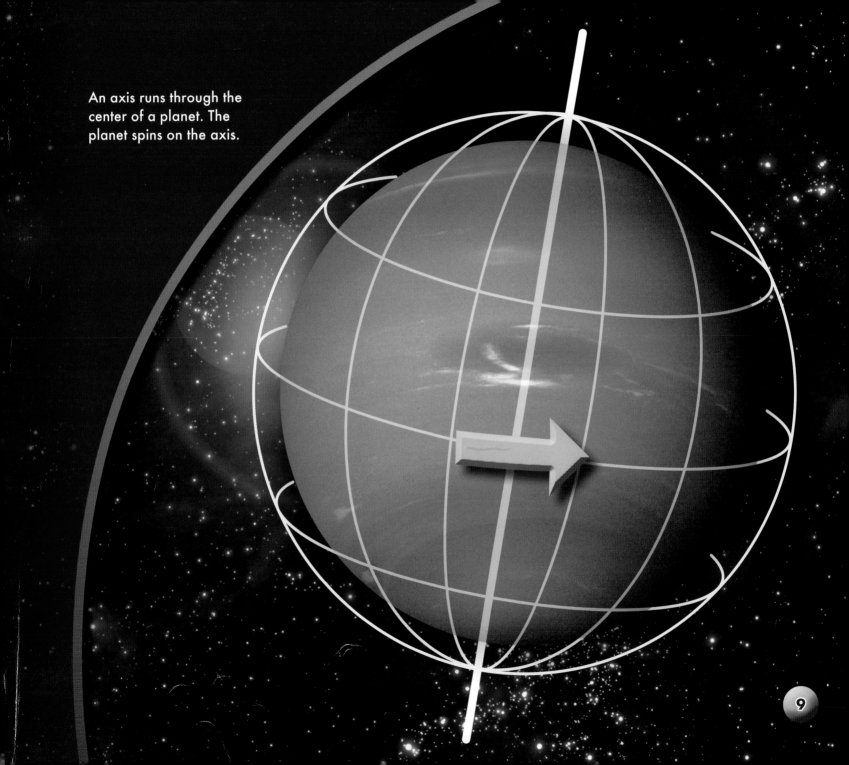

An axis runs through the center of a planet. The planet spins on the axis.

Neptune is far out in the solar system. It takes the planet a long time to orbit the sun. A year is the time it takes for a planet to travel around the sun once. One year on Neptune equals 165 Earth years. Neptune has only orbited the sun once since it was discovered!

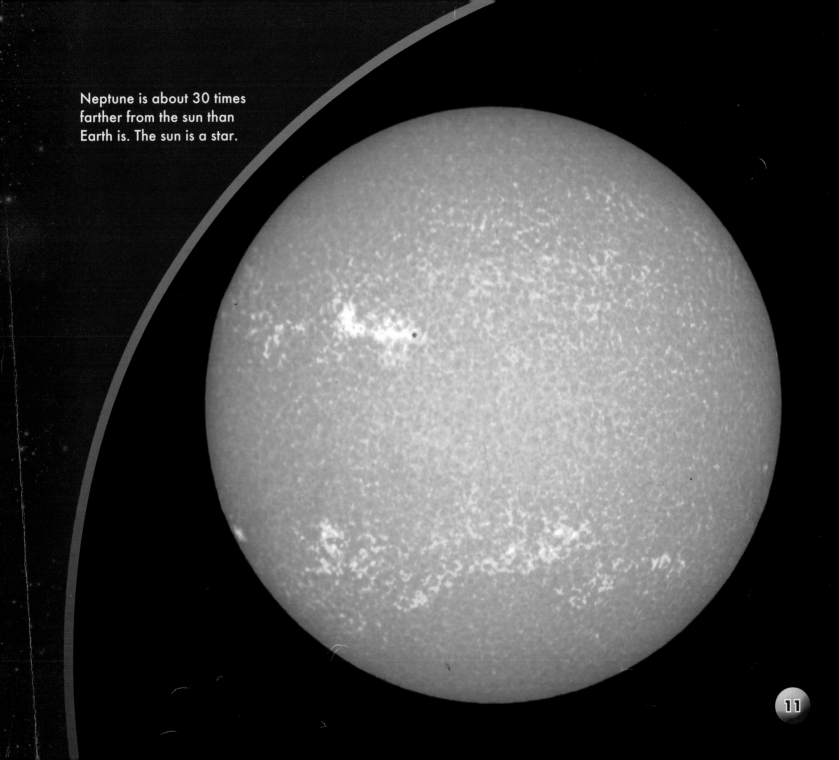

Neptune is about 30 times
farther from the sun than
Earth is. The sun is a star.

11

Finding Neptune

About 2,000 years ago, Romans named the planets Mercury, Venus, Mars, Jupiter, and Saturn after their gods. They could see these planets in the night sky.

But Neptune wasn't discovered until 1846. It is too far away for us to see without a **telescope**.

Uranus (YOOR-uh-nuss) is the seventh planet from the sun. Scientists found it just 65 years before they discovered Neptune.

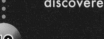

Planets closer to the sun than Neptune, such as Venus (top) and Jupiter, can be seen from Earth without a telescope.

Venus

Jupiter

Scientists knew Neptune existed before they saw it. How? They noticed a change in Uranus's orbit. That told them strong **gravity** from another planet was pulling on Uranus. So they started looking for another planet. Johann G. Galle spotted Neptune with a telescope on September 23, 1846.

Fun Fact

Galileo Galilei almost discovered the planet Neptune in 1612. But his early telescope had not been perfected yet. Looking through it, he thought Neptune was just a star.

John Couch Adams was one of the scientists who helped find Neptune.

This new planet needed a name. Some called it "the planet outside Uranus." One idea was Janus, the Roman god of gates. Another was Oceanus, a river that once was believed to circle the world.

Soon, scientists around the world agreed. Because of its blue color, they named it after the Roman god of the sea—Neptune.

It was believed that the Roman god Neptune could cause storms at sea.

Layers of Gas

Neptune is a **gas** giant. It is made mostly of gas and some liquid with no solid surface. Other planets have rocky, hard surfaces with volcanoes and mountains.

Fun Fact

There are two types of planets.

TERRESTRIAL PLANETS (mostly rock) are close to the sun. They are: Mercury, Venus, Earth, and Mars.

GAS GIANTS (mostly gas and liquid) are farther from the sun. They are: Jupiter, Saturn, Uranus, and Neptune.

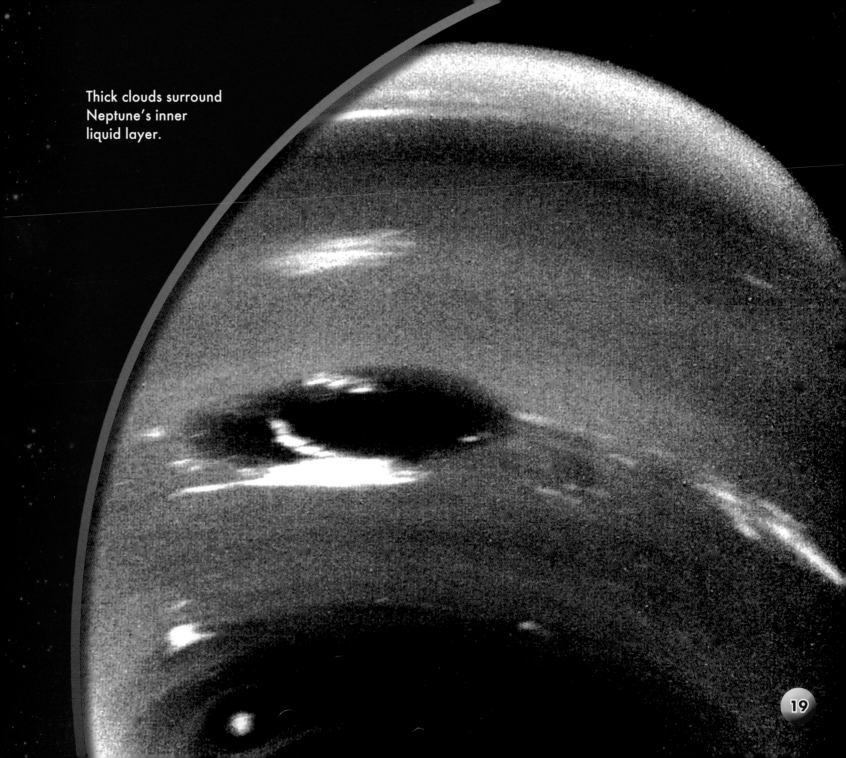

Thick clouds surround Neptune's inner liquid layer.

19

A Closer Look

What's it like on Neptune? No one has ever walked on the planet. Remember—there's no hard surface!

Scientists use strong telescopes to **observe** Neptune from Earth. In space, NASA spacecraft collect **data** and take pictures. These show that more than ten moons orbit Neptune. The planet has six rings that slightly glow.

Fun Fact

NASA stands for the National Aeronautics and Space Administration. It is a US agency that studies space and the planets.

The *Voyager 2* spacecraft took detailed images of Neptune's rings.

In 1989, *Voyager 2* was the first spacecraft to reach Neptune. It flew as close as 3,000 miles (4,800 km) above Neptune's north pole. That mission gave us much of the information we have about the planet. *Voyager 2* discovered six of Neptune's moons.

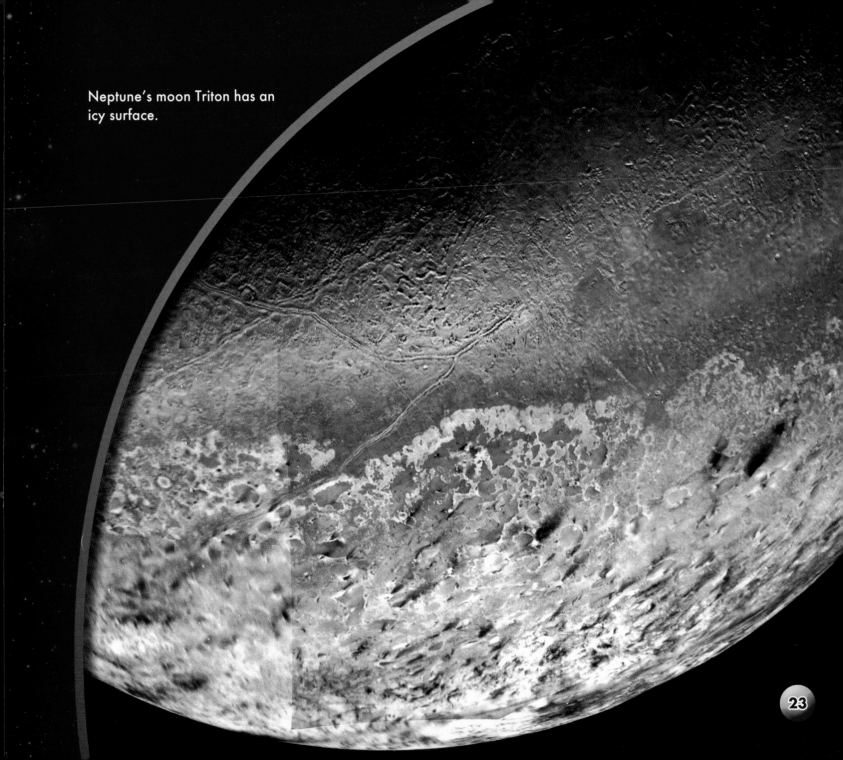

Neptune's moon Triton has an icy surface.

23

A planet's **atmosphere** is the layer of gas around it. Earth's atmosphere is the air we breathe. Neptune's atmosphere contains methane and other gases. On Earth, we use methane to help run our cars and heat our homes.

Thick, bright clouds swirl over Neptune. The planet is dark, stormy, and very cold. The average temperature is –353°F (–214°C). That's almost three times colder than Earth's coldest temperature! Because Neptune is so far from the sun, it's dark there, even during the day.

Fun Fact

It takes light from the sun more than four hours to reach Neptune.

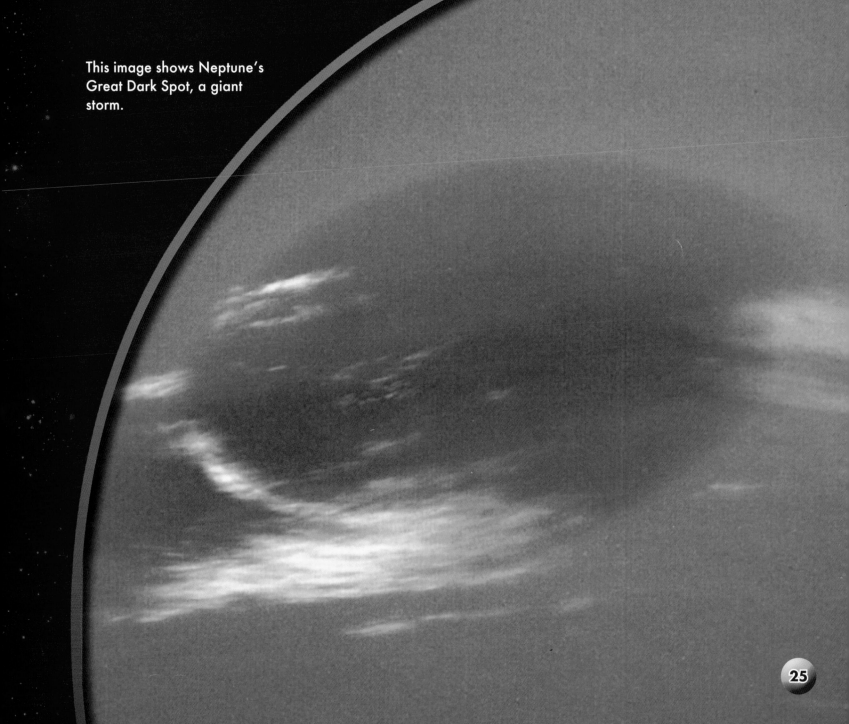

This image shows Neptune's Great Dark Spot, a giant storm.

What Neptune Can Tell Us

All living things on Earth need water. That's why scientists look for water on other planets. They might find living things in other places in our solar system.

Neptune is partly made of water. But we haven't found life there. In the future, scientists will recreate the conditions on Neptune in a lab. They will study how water behaves. They might learn how life could exist outside Earth.

Scientists study cloud streaks and patterns in Neptune's atmosphere.

In 2010, scientists found a rocky **asteroid** following Neptune's orbit. The asteroid's position might give us new clues about how the solar system formed. Scientists are excited to see what Neptune will teach us next.

Scientists hope to learn more about distant Neptune, the farthest planet from the sun in our solar system.

Neptune

Triton

GLOSSARY

asteroid (ASS-tuh-roid): An asteroid is a rock that orbits the sun. Scientists discovered an asteroid that follows Neptune's orbit.

atmosphere (AT-muhss-fihr): An atmosphere is the mixture of gases around a planet or a star. Scientists study Neptune's atmosphere to learn more about the planet.

axis (AK-siss): An axis is an imaginary line that runs through the center of a planet or a moon. Neptune rotates on its axis.

data (DAY-tuh): Data are facts, figures, and other information. Scientists hope to learn more data about Neptune.

dwarf planets (DWORF PLAN-itz): Dwarf planets are round bodies in space that orbit the sun, are not moons, and are not large enough to clear away their paths around the sun. Dwarf planets often have similar objects that orbit near them.

gas (GASS): A gas is a substance that moves around freely and can spread out. Neptune is made mostly of gas and liquid.

gravity (GRAV-uh-tee): Gravity is a force that pulls objects toward each other. Neptune was discovered because its gravity was changing Uranus's orbit.

observe (uhb-ZURV): To observe is to watch and study something closely. Scientists use strong telescopes to observe Neptune.

orbit (OR-bit): To orbit is to travel around another body in space, often in an oval path. Planets orbit the sun.

solar system (SOH-lur SISS-tum): Our solar system is made up of the sun, eight planets and their moons, and smaller bodies that orbit the sun. Neptune is the eighth planet from the sun in our solar system.

telescope (TEL-uh-skope): A telescope is a tool that makes faraway objects appear closer. Neptune cannot be seen without a telescope.

FURTHER INFORMATION

BOOKS

Landau, Elaine. *Neptune*. New York: Children's Press, 2008.

Sherman, Josepha. *Neptune*. New York: Marshall Cavendish Benchmark, 2010.

Trammel, Howard K. *The Solar System*. New York: Children's Press, 2010.

WEB SITES

Visit our Web site for links about Neptune: **childsworld.com/links**

Note to Parents, Teachers, and Librarians: We routinely verify our Web links to make sure they are safe and active sites. So encourage your readers to check them out!

INDEX

ABOUT THE AUTHOR

L. L. Owens has been writing books for children since 1998. She writes both fiction and nonfiction and especially loves helping kids explore the world around them.